# WINNING THE RACE

WINNING THE RACE
Clearing the Hurdles to a Meaningful Retirement



ISBN: 978-1-964046-52-5

The information provided in this book is for informational purposes only and is not intended to be a source of advice or credit analysis with respect to the material presented. The information and/or documents contained in this book do not constitute legal or financial advice and should never be used without first consulting with an insurance and/or a financial professional to determine what may be best for your individual needs.

The publisher and the author do not make any guarantee or other promise as to any results that may be obtained from using the content of this book. You should never make any investment decision without first consulting with your own financial advisor and conducting your own research and due diligence. To the maximum extent permitted by law, the publisher and the author disclaim any and all liability in the event any information, commentary, analysis, opinions, advice, and/or recommendations contained in this book prove to be inaccurate, incomplete, or unreliable or result in any investment or other losses.

Although the author and publisher have made every effort to ensure that the information in this book was correct at press time, the author and publisher do not assume and hereby disclaim any liability to any party for any loss, damage, or disruption caused by errors or omissions, whether such errors or omissions result from negligence, accident, or any other cause.

Content contained or made available through this book is not intended to and does not constitute legal advice or investment advice, and no attorney-client relationship is formed. The publisher and the author are providing this book and its contents on an "as is" basis. Your use of the information in this book is at your own risk.

Editing by Ryan Huber
Copyediting by Heather Skaggs
Proofreading by Geena Barret
Text design and composition by Emily Fritz
Cover design by Casey Fritz

# WINNING THE RACE

Clearing the Hurdles to a Meaningful Retirement

**TIM DAVIS, RICP®, CLU®, CEBS**

Certified Financial Fiduciary®

*I dedicate this book to my clients, both present and future. May you enter retirement with less worry, have time to reflect, enjoy the rewards of your working years, nurture relationships, contribute to your communities, be productive—and be happy.*

# Contents

# FOREWORD

Writing the foreword for Tim's new book, *Winning the Race*, is an honor. Not often in life do you have the opportunity to meet people of impeccable quality, but Tim is just such a person. The words in his book are much more than a guiding arrow; they are the words of a wholly committed human whose joy in life is always to make the other person better. His book does just that; it has made me a better person.

As Tim states, winning is a feeling that stays with you forever. It carries the joy of achievement, the pride of hard work, and the satisfaction of seeing your efforts come to fruition. Life is a race filled with hurdles, and how you approach those challenges determines how strong you finish.

Much like hurdling, life is a series of strides punctuated by challenges. Each hurdle tests your timing, focus, and determination. He learned early that success wasn't just about speed—it was about strategy, preparation, and the ability to clear obstacles while maintaining momentum. Those lessons, honed on the track, became the foundation of his approach to life and, later, his career as a financial professional. Now, in *Winning the Race*, he shares how those principles of hurdling can guide you through one of life's greatest races: retirement.

Every race begins at the starting blocks, where careful preparation and a strong launch set the tone. For most of us, the early stretches of life's race are about building—careers, families, and wealth. But as we approach retirement, we enter the final stretch, where the hurdles can be larger and the stakes higher. In this critical phase, it's not just about running fast; it's about running smart. The hurdles of retirement—rising healthcare costs, market volatility, and the risk of outliving your savings—require careful planning and execution. This book is your guide to clearing those hurdles with confidence and ensuring you finish strong.

Tim also adds a new dimension to the art of retirement by integrating guarantees into retirement planning. As his career progressed, he became aware of the importance of incorporating guarantees into practical planning. His vehicle is fixed indexed annuities, where guaranteed income can be translated into real life. Knowing that your income is there and nothing can change has helped Tim's clientele reduce stress and gain true financial freedom.

Tim tells the story through his personal experiences as a track star, a husband, a father, and a grandfather in common-sense language and in a manner that is easily understood.

Well done, truly a First Place share!

—**BILL BROICH**,
Founder of Annuity.com,
Calistoga, California

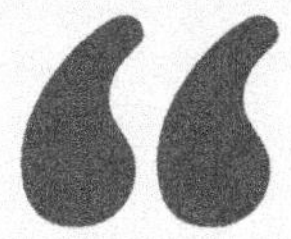

I know what it's like to go back to the starting blocks to run the race to financial security all over again.

# INTRODUCTION

## The Finish Line

I know what it feels like to win.

Many years ago, as a senior at Wharton High School, I was a standout hurdler. I won so much, I was offered a scholarship to the University of Texas to run track as a Longhorn. They say you can't coach speed, and for me, running hurdles just came naturally. I was fast, I had a natural stride, and I quickly got used to being in the lead. The feeling of coming out of the blocks, spikes digging into the orange chipped-brick surface of the track, taking each hurdle in stride, and seeing no one ahead of me or even beside me was hard to beat. The all-out sprint after I cleared the last hurdle, the feeling of breaking the tape—it was nothing short of exhilarating.

I've won in other areas of my life: I've built several successful businesses, worked with my wife to cultivate a great marriage, and raised six wonderful daughters. And now I get to enjoy my grandchildren in the golden years of my sprint around the sun. There have been a lot of wins for me. I'm blessed.

I also know what it feels like to lose—to fall in the packed orange dirt, to relinquish your chance to be a champion, to come up lame, to watch the lead slip out of your grasp. It's devastating. I know what it's like to realize the college game is another level above even the most elite high school competitions. I know what it's like to lose a twin brother, and I know what it's like to see everything you've worked so hard for come crashing down in a series of risky investments. I know what it's like to go back to the starting blocks to run the race to financial security all over again.

If you're reading this book, you probably know what it's like to win, too, and you know how much there is to lose. As you're entering that final sprint, heading toward or already enjoying the fruits of your labor in retirement, you don't want to see it all come crashing down. You want to "hold the lead" against the unpredictability of a crazy, ever-changing world. That's why I wrote this book: to help you do just that.

I want you to enjoy this final sprint called retirement, to rest easy knowing you'll stay in the lead. I want you to live freely and enjoy this season, not spend all day worrying about what might happen. I help people plan, stretch their resources if need be, protect their winnings, and sustain their legacy when their race is done. I do it by helping them translate part of what they have into "safe money," combinations of annuities that protect a portion of their assets and guarantee a certain level of income for life. I wrote this book to share what I've learned with you, to help answer some of the questions you might have about retirement planning and annuities, just like I've been able to help so many of my clients over the years. My goal is to help you clear the hurdles to a meaningful retirement, to lean into that final sprint so that you can be confident you're finishing strong.

If you're interested in that kind of retirement, if you want to protect your victories against loss, risk, timing, and more, then keep reading. We're just warming up.

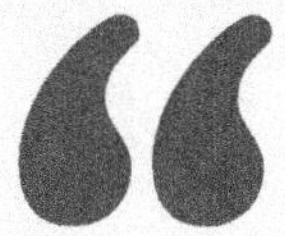

Having a high risk tolerance is a big help in starting and growing businesses, and it was very beneficial to me.

CHAPTER 1

# Clearing the Hurdle of Loss

The clearest way to think about retirement is to think about the ways in which you can clear the hurdle of loss. In other words, how do you protect your winnings and prevent the kind of loss that stops you in your tracks and puts a meaningful retirement out of reach?

## Losing Everything

To lose everything, you have to have something to lose, and I certainly did.

Relatively early in my career, after ten years as a life insurance agent, I wanted to build something that would produce an income and also grow as an asset. I was looking for something like the property and casualty business, whose agents sell businesses. A lot of the guys who build these property and casualty agencies sell them to pay for their retirement. As a life insurance agent, however, especially at the time, I didn't have that option; we were just commission-based salespeople. So ten years out of college, I started my first company and built it up over time. I had a business partner, and after four to five years in business, we sold it to Hospital Corporation of America (HCA) and made a pretty decent sum of money for a couple of guys in the first part of their careers.

Because of the way HCA managed the business, we ended up buying it back five years later for pennies on the dollar, then selling it again not too long after that. I started a brokerage and consulting firm, and we bought a dental HMO and sold it to Protective Life for a really nice exit (sale of the business). So I had four good exits. I say all this because, as an entrepreneur, I had the optimism and confidence to go into a number of ventures. My first one was a start-up with a $10,000 investment, and we turned that into seven figures. Having a high risk tolerance is a big help in starting and growing businesses, and it was very beneficial to me.

Once I had sold those companies and took a form of very early retirement, I figured I had done it so well that I'd invest in several cutting-edge start-ups. I expected at least a couple of them to go to the moon. It turned out the timing was terrible; the kinds of innovative companies I was investing in were starting to fail, one after another. Capital

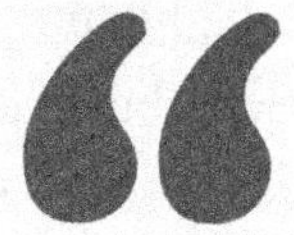

They can protect their wins and prevent a devastating loss because the totally preventable kind of loss is the biggest hurdle to a meaningful retirement.

dried up seemingly overnight, and it was just awful. I still had that high risk tolerance, but it didn't serve me very well in managing my money. I broke all the rules, and the reality behind those rules broke me. More accurately, it broke my bank account.

You see, the irony is the things that had made me such a success and led to big wins in my life were the same things that cost me everything I had worked for, at least financially. An entrepreneurial spirit, a high risk tolerance, a focus on growth, a track record of success, and the willingness to ignore many of the unknowns became tragic flaws as I tried to protect and preserve my successes over the course of my career.

The good news is that I was able to look myself in the mirror, take responsibility for my foolishness, and put my entrepreneurial running shoes back on. I was able to recover from a serious financial injury. It wasn't easy, and it wasn't a whole lot of fun in the beginning, but I learned some valuable lessons about life, growth, and especially loss. Those are the lessons I share with people today so they don't have to go through what I went through. They can protect their wins and prevent a devastating loss because the totally preventable kind of loss is the biggest hurdle to a meaningful retirement.

## What Is the Hurdle of Loss?

It might seem obvious, but when we talk about this kind of loss, we're talking about failure. This isn't an act of God but a series of choices we make about how to plan and prepare for retirement. This kind of loss results from a failure to protect, to diversify, to consider the unknowns of the future. It might seem harsh, but I can tell you from personal experience that tripping over the hurdle of loss when it comes to retirement is almost always preventable if you're willing to think about it in advance.

This hurdle is also a kind of feeling, an absence not only of what you had but of the life and retirement you dreamed of. That's why it's so important to look ahead to it today, to live in reality and make the changes necessary to clear this hurdle now.

## Why Is Loss a Hurdle?

This question has the most obvious answer in the whole book, at least on the surface, but it may not be obvious to everyone in the moment. That might explain why the hurdle of loss is so common for people in the run-up to and the beginning of their retirement. Loss is a hurdle because it can, and often does, happen unexpectedly. It destroys what you've worked for over a long period, but many times there are no obvious warning signs that loss is on the way. We all know loss is a hurdle once it's happened, but many people just don't want to think about it or do what it takes to prevent loss before the awful moment it arrives. Because in the end, preventing loss is far easier than recovering from it.

### *How Do I Prevent Loss?*

First, we have to recognize the reality of the hurdle; it exists even when we can't see it because the nature of preventable loss is that it's hidden in the fog of the future. We do have principles for preventing loss, though:

- Don't try for maximum return.
- Have a plan and a structure in place.
- Diversify your life and your principal as much as you can.

After all, some losses you can't prevent (such as personal loss, some health problems, and natural disasters), so you need to prevent the ones you can while you still can. The other track involves recovering from loss, and it's often a much more difficult, sometimes seemingly impossible, race to win.

### *How Do I Recover from Loss?*

You can recover from some kinds of loss, but it's much harder than preventing loss in the first place. First you face

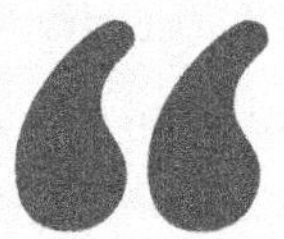

I found my way to help other people protect themselves from a similar hurdle: by using the financial tool of annuities.

reality, like I did when I lost almost everything. Then you have to take responsibility and put your running shoes back on, which is an option for some, like me, but unfortunately doesn't work for everyone. Again, you can recover from the kinds of loss we're talking about here, but there are no guarantees. Many people simply don't find their way forward once they've tripped over such a massive hurdle to their retirement. Fortunately, for most people, there's still time to get ready and clear the hurdle of loss rather than having to recover from it.

## How Do We Clear the Hurdle?

Even if you agree with me so far, you might be thinking, *That's great life advice, Tim, but how does it actually work?* After my big loss, I found my way to help other people protect themselves from a similar hurdle: by using the financial tool of annuities.

An annuity is a contract between you and an insurance company. There are many types of annuities and literally hundreds of products offered in the marketplace. The traditional annuity, first used thousands of years ago, provides for a lifetime income that ends at death. These plans are similar to the incomes provided by pensions, which are much less common today than they were decades ago.

Most annuities are either fixed or variable. The account values in variable annuities are invested in mutual funds, which can subject the owner to a loss of principal. Variable annuities also carry significant fees, which can adversely impact potential growth.

There are two categories of fixed annuities. The first includes fixed annuities that provide a fixed guaranteed rate for a specific period of time. The second consists of annuities that offer interest credited based on stock market indices such as the S&P 500 without actually being invested in the market. These in the second category are called fixed indexed annuities (FIAs). I most frequently use FIAs in various forms to satisfy my clients' need for safety, growth, and the provision of a lifetime income.

Actually, since their terms can vary, annuities are more like an entire toolbox than a single tool, which we'll explore in the pages that follow. The bottom line, however, is that annuities help prevent loss by protecting your principal or maximizing it through asset diversification. In many situations, this means annuities help protect you from loss by providing a guaranteed lifetime income. We sometimes use an approach called laddering, in which that income can be deferred and allowed to grow until you really need it. We're going to dig into the details below, but the major difference between annuities and other, riskier investments or retirement plans is that with annuities, you're not banking on probabilities and unknowns but on guarantees.

For example, some fixed indexed annuities are geared toward growth, but they protect your principal at the same time, which means you can't lose money. You can still earn meaningful interest, but there are no fees, and you even maintain some liquidity. For some people, growth annuities are a better option for a portion of their principal, but for others, income annuities make more sense. Frequently, a combination of both is deployed to optimize a plan. I'm independent, which is important, so I can give the best advice for you, and I'm not tied to any particular product or company. I can help you select among the many options in the marketplace, and we can find the best fit so that you can clear the hurdle of loss and cross the finish line to a meaningful retirement.

Think of this as your personal pension plan. We can set up a structure, a plan, and a system to maximize your retirement while preventing loss. We can also mitigate inflation by laddering fixed incomes from annuities over time; there are endless combinations of annuities we might use to clear the hurdle.

## Mr. and Mrs. Tobias Go to . . . Wherever They Want

A few years ago, I was able to help a couple who wanted to be prepared for a meaningful retirement and needed to clear the hurdle of loss. Mr. and Mrs. Tobias[1] came to me looking for peace of mind and a way to protect what they had worked for over the years.

Mr. Tobias was a machinist at a manufacturing company, and he was making a good salary. Machinists tend to make really good money working for the same company for many years. The company had a nice match as part of its retirement program. He had accumulated over a million dollars in his account, and he and his wife lived frugally, within their means. Their house was paid for and they were

1 Not their actual names; all names and some details have been changed to protect the innocent.

in good health, looking forward to traveling in the RV they had bought. That was their splurge; they planned to spend a lot of time on the road and told me that they just didn't want to lose money.

I worked with them to structure a combination of their assets and income, starting with Social Security. We put together a program to optimize their Social Security by helping them choose the best time to start claiming it as income. In addition, we placed a portion of their retirement funds in safe money, rolling it out of their 401(k) plan and into an annuity that paid them a lifetime income, jointly. It will pay for the rest of their lives and increase over time based on the performance of an index.

Additionally, we put another significant amount of their retirement savings into an indexed annuity that was designed for safety and growth. No fees, no income produced, no guaranteed income, just an account from which they could draw to supplement their income. Finally, we left some money with an advisor who was still investing in some equities for them, which amounted to about a third of their money still invested in the market. And this combination of measures did everything they needed it to do.

Once we put that plan together and into motion, the feedback I got from them was incredibly satisfying. I was able to give Mr. and Mrs. Tobias a complete breakdown of where this money, their income, would come from going forward. I was able to assure them that they would never run out of money and could enjoy a stress-free retirement on the road. They don't have to watch the stock market and worry about whether the income that should be deposited next month would be there or not because the performance of their managed account wasn't critical to the overall success of their plan or their income. That portion was designated for luxuries, for extras rather than necessities, strictly speaking.

The relief they expressed was moving: The idea that they could lock the house up, get in the RV, and hit the road for weeks at a time gave them so much comfort. They left with big smiles on their faces. In this real-life case, it was really meaningful to me to get that kind of feedback, to see the plan we had made put them in a worry-free position. They would have enough money to enjoy their retirement, travel, relax, and spend time with their grandkids without the worry of losing their money or running out. And that's how Mr. and Mrs. Tobias cleared the hurdle of loss.

## Next Steps

If you have reached or are nearing retirement, which is what I call the end of your "accumulation phase," then it's time to evaluate your sources of income in retirement, evaluate your risk of loss, consider giving up possible returns for definite safety, and protect what you've built. I'm here to help you do just that. If you want to retire without spending that retirement worrying about losing it all, you need to take steps to mitigate loss today.

You may not think of your life or your retirement in terms of loss; it may seem too "black and white" to frame preparation for retirement in those terms. Perhaps that's not how you think. I certainly didn't. It may be more helpful to think about your approach to retirement as clearing the hurdle of risk instead.

# CHAPTER 2

# Clearing the Hurdle of Risk

One way to think about preparing for retirement is to put a plan in place to prevent loss, but that's not the only way to run the race. For many people, the hurdle of risk is what they see coming up between them and a meaningful retirement. Often people have gained a lot by taking risks in the past, and as retirement approaches, some part of them knows they need to adjust the amount of risk they're taking on to consolidate and protect those gains for retirement. In other words, as you plan for the end of your full-time working years, how do you right-size your risk?

## Building Businesses from Nothing

When I started my first real entrepreneurial endeavor, when I stepped away from a "normal" job into my first venture, I was excited and optimistic. Now, it wasn't a complete break because I had spent ten years in the life insurance business. I had been writing more and more group insurance, which does provide recurring revenue.

So while I wasn't in a position where someone was paying me a salary, I had positioned myself to receive recurring revenue on my employee benefits book of business, and I still had the ability to sell more that generated commissions for income, so I didn't have to jump off a cliff and start completely from zero. But it was still a leap.

My business partner came from a salaried position and had to live on his savings. Our endeavor was a third-party administration (TPA) business. We had already started selling employers on the concept of self-funding their employee benefits, so we were just going to add our TPA instead of a competing TPA that we didn't think was doing a good job (and there was no viable alternative on offer). So part of the strategy was defensive, and part of it was opportunistic. We felt like the opportunity was there, and it turned out that it absolutely was because there wasn't much competition in the market. We had existing business that we could move into and change the administration to our TPA. Because of all this, there were synergies involved in the start-up, and we didn't go into it blindly. We felt like we had a good starting position, the market was right for it, and the timing was good. Because of all this, I wasn't scared at all. I was encouraged.

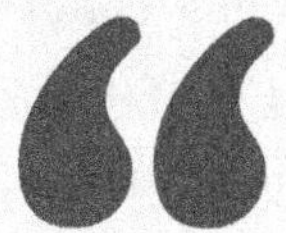

We were creating something from nothing, and we were succeeding at it.

I did have four young children at home, and people were asking me, "What in the world are you doing?" That didn't bother me. Thank goodness my wife trusted me and believed we were going to be fine, and it worked out great for us. In the early days, we worked our tails off; I'd wake up at night and make notes of ideas and things related to the business. I didn't want to forget them, so I had a little dictation machine, and I'd go in the closet and talk into it about things to do the next day and things to check into. It was exhilarating. We were creating something from nothing, and we were succeeding at it.

It was still stressful because we were going ninety miles an hour to make it work. Interestingly enough, if you have a partner in the business, you have somebody to hold you accountable, and that goes both ways. There definitely has to be an element of trust, and in this case it worked out well. Not all of my partnerships worked out, but more did than didn't, so I don't discourage people from having business partnerships. You'll hear people say not to take on partners, but it depends. If you contribute different things and it's the old "one plus one equals three," then it's worthwhile.

After twelve to eighteen months, we started to feel like we had done it; we took a risk, it was working, and we were going to see the fruits of our labors. However, that risk tolerance, confidence, entrepreneurship, optimism—those things that make us successful at the beginning of our earning years and that worked so well for me as a younger entrepreneur—start threatening to become real weaknesses, even blind spots, as we approach retirement.

After years of building businesses and several successful exits, I became the same kind of investor as I took steps away from running businesses on a day-to-day basis: confident, optimistic, bold, and willing to take a risk. When I left the insurance business, I had a pretty decent stack of chips. The people pitching these early-stage companies for investments reminded me of myself as a rising entrepreneur—they all seemed like they had a well-thought-out business plan, and the market seemed right for it. As it turns out, it wasn't.

I had a kind of kinship with the entrepreneurs who were starting these companies, and I figured since I had done it, they should be able to do it too. I also wasn't going to put all my eggs in one basket, but I did go too far for too long with one company, and I lost. That was the big loss. It was a lot of money. It just didn't pan out.

If I could talk to that version of myself today, I would tell him, "You're taking too much risk with too much of your portfolio." I should have limited my investment to either a percentage or a dollar amount and drawn the line there. Experts say that with risky investing, you write down what you're willing to risk on it, and you don't deviate. With the big loss, I just kept feeding it and really believing in it, and it reached a point where I reasoned, *Well, I've got this much into it. I need to keep investing so I'll be there when they do finally make it.* I would tell my younger self to set a limit, diversify, and not go headlong into one type of asset, like start-ups and high-risk investments. Be conservative with a large portion of it, something like 75 percent. That would have left me in a much different position.

However, knowing my younger self, I suspect he would have said, "Sir, with all due respect, I hear what you're saying, but I'm pretty good at this. I've had some major successes here. What's going to change? I've done a good job with my financial life. I've built things. I've saved."

What I would tell him, and what I've helped others to see, is that you have to be more honest about the risks you're taking. This is not a game, and you don't want to gamble your entire future. There was a time when I could have salvaged a good bit. I didn't have to lose everything. But I didn't pay heed to that voice in the back of my head, the angel on my shoulder who was telling me, "You've crossed the line. You need to stop." Even if I had lost 25 percent of my assets, that would have been a different story. I could have recovered a lot more easily. I needed to push back against those tendencies that had made me successful earlier in my career. I needed to right-size my risk.

## What Is the Hurdle of Risk?

The hurdle of risk is the reality that most people need to adjust or calibrate their risk as they approach retirement. I say "calibrate" rather than "eliminate" because risk can't be fully eliminated from most of our lives, and a lot of us still want to take some calculated risks, even in retirement. For many of us, risk was necessary, even helpful, in getting to where we are in the first place. The questions are "How much risk, and when?"

There are also differences in each person's risk tolerance, the amount they can actually live with. We all live somewhere on the spectrum between excitement and safety, adventure and security. To clear the hurdle of risk, we need to fine-tune and right-size our approach to it so that later in our lives, we've put a portion of our principal into "safe money." Safe money options still let us take some risks but empower us to keep them at an appropriate level.

## Why Is Risk a Hurdle?

Risk is a hurdle because it's impossible to avoid entirely, because life would be too boring for many of us without it, and because everyone has a different personal risk tolerance.

For example, I happen to have most of the classic characteristics of an entrepreneur, so I also have a higher risk tolerance than the average person. On day one of a complete start-up, there's no revenue, only expenses, so it does require a high risk tolerance, and some people would be totally paralyzed at the thought of making that leap. One thing I help my clients with is measuring risk tolerance, and there are a few different ways to go about that, which I'll explore later in this chapter.

There's another factor to consider in risk tolerance: More often than not, people "talk" a higher risk tolerance than they actually have, saying things like "Oh yeah, I could take a loss if the market has a hiccup or something." Many people think they can withstand that until it happens, and then panic sets in as they realize the situation is serious and this is real life. People need to assess themselves honestly and recognize how much risk of losing their retirement principal they can assume without panic and worry setting in. I help people walk through this process as well.

The whole idea of enjoying a meaningful retirement, to the extent you can position your assets and provide for an income that covers your basic and discretionary needs, is related to how you handle or tolerate risk. Many people worry about the possibility of some event that would cause them to lose principal, jeopardize their lifestyle, or force them to make significant changes. That's the risk you want to mitigate, and it's what I try to help people recognize, realize, visualize, and feel—what it would be like if you enter retirement relying on risky investments and they don't work out very well.

### *What Risks Are Worth Taking?*

This raises the question: What risks are worth taking for you? Your answer will depend on your age, personality, assets, target retirement age, and the kind of retirement you envision.

When it comes to personality, for many people, there's something boring about safety and therefore something boring about annuities. Safety doesn't give the kind of juice and excitement some people are looking for. These people are *risk tolerators*, but many of us need to be *risk managers*,

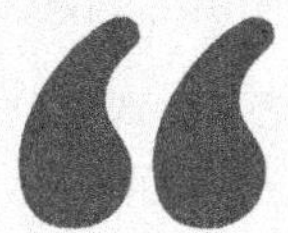

Risk management requires an adult in the room to make decisions based on recognition of those consequences.

especially as retirement approaches. The first step to managing your risk in a way that fits your personality is to be honest with yourself. When I made all those aggressive investments, I wasn't being honest about the true consequences. I was ignoring, instead of recognizing, the consequences of a potential bad outcome.

If we can honestly acknowledge what the consequences could be, if we can visualize our lives if the outcome turned out to be the worst, we can keep from fooling ourselves. Risk management requires an adult in the room to make decisions based on recognition of those consequences. I'm guilty of wanting the sexy return, something exciting, because I was always bored with the approach of plodding along, saving from income. It's a difficult mindset switch for people like me.

All of this requires discipline. I think I'm disciplined to a point, but I was undisciplined about forcing myself to face the worst-case scenario of my risk tolerance. Now, you don't need to choose between 0 percent risk and 100 percent risk; depending on your situation approaching retirement, there's plenty of middle ground between the safe, boring path and the foolish, risky path.

A lot of it depends on how much you have available. Do you have enough to allocate some to safe money, keep from hitting rock bottom, and set aside another portion that would give you the juice, the thrill, without exposing the entire pile of money to loss? It's a matter of finding the middle ground if that's possible for you, but you can't risk losing it all; that's just foolish. It's reckless. Again, I should know.

Depending on your assets, for most people who want to keep some skin in the risk game, I recommend keeping somewhere between 10 percent and 25 percent in the market. It wouldn't be the most prudent path, but if a person's wired that way, feed that beast to a certain point, but draw a line. You have to draw an absolute line. That's when having a third party, a gatekeeper, to manage that smaller portion can be very helpful. Get somebody who will carry out a plan like you know you should. They don't have to be a wealth management expert, but having a gatekeeper is one way to keep out of trouble.

Before you do any of this, though, before you manage and calibrate your risk, you need to figure out your actual risk tolerance. We'll explore the details of this crucial first step below.

### *How Can I Protect Myself from the Downside of Risk?*

The first thing you need to protect yourself from the downside of risk is a plan. You can't wander into a meaningful retirement. A plan will help you transition from just tolerating risk to actively managing it through diversification and placing a portion of your principal into safe money. Before you can take any action, though, you need a clear picture of who you are, your actual risk tolerance, the assets at your disposal, and the methods you can use to clear the hurdle of risk. Let's get into the details.

## How Do We Clear the Hurdle?

To clear the hurdle of risk, we first have to be honest about our risk tolerance. I use tools like the RISA (Retirement Income Style Awareness®) to help people take that first step. The RISA is a risk profile for people's approach to retirement income. It's not necessarily for a thirty-five-year-old to take; it's designed for a person approaching retirement or in retirement. Wade Pfau created it with a partner. For twenty years or so, he was the head of the retirement income planning department at the American College of Financial Services. He holds a PhD, and he knows what he's talking about.

The RISA is a useful tool because it gives you a report based on your answers to questions about how you would like to see your retirement income being generated, whether your tendency would be to fully invest and make withdrawals for income, choose the other extreme of guaranteed lifetime income based on all your principal, or something in between. The tool plots the results on a grid, but then it gives a narrative based on those types, suggesting the best fit of a combination of approaches to funding retirement income. It's a really helpful tool, and like all tools, its recommendation is not necessarily the only answer. It can be very helpful for couples because the two spouses often have totally different profiles.

More often than not, the wife doesn't want to risk anything. The men tend to be more cavalier: "Yeah, I can make it," they say. "We'll be fine." My team and I often have to help couples walk through that difference and find a compromise in the plan we put together for them. Most times, we can arrange a certain level of guaranteed lifelong income in addition to Social Security.

Social Security is indexed for cost of living. That provides a base of income. Then, if one spouse wants to invest and generate more income with their retirement savings, and if the other spouse agrees, there are all kinds of ways to invest it. It helps to put multiple pieces together to generate income because no two people are alike. Study after study, even making its way into the Wall Street crowd, has acknowledged the satisfaction generated when people have a floor of guaranteed income for life.

These studies are concluding that people are happier with some level of guarantee. Part of my job is to communicate that to clients, to help them realize and visualize just how beneficial and how comforting it is to know that every month there will be a deposit in your checking account. Social Security and annuity income combined is what we call a "personal pension plan." When you have one of these, you can assume a little more risk with your other investments, not to lose it all but to seek a higher return. That's the kind of counseling that goes into discussing how each person feels, and the RISA survey helps everyone get on the same page. Then we can right-size their risk with a number of tools at our disposal.

Now, I'm an advisor who helps people with safe money. I offer annuities, but I also know about other methods that can bring my clients peace of mind, help them plan, and put their mind at ease when it comes to right-sizing risk. Of course, we use guaranteed lifetime income to mitigate the risk of loss of principal that will later be used for income, and we want to make sure they have a reliable source of income as long as they live. But there are other considerations, and other tools, that many clients use to clear the hurdle of risk.

First of all, I don't recommend bonds. Bonds are not a good fit in the portfolio because there are better ways of doing the same thing. Even growth annuities offer many of the characteristics of bonds without the downside. There are also alternative investments. Some conservative private investments in different types of real estate have a higher degree of security, such as multifamily apartments. I happen to know someone who handles those kinds of investments and is very disciplined. You have to be careful about who you trust with your money, but there are opportunities out there. Find a disciplined manager who doesn't overpay and treats their investors fairly. You can generate recurring revenue, a nice source of income, but with an upside potential for capital gains. These are private partnerships, but they require an accredited investor. One downside is that they don't have a lot of liquidity. You can't get cash out whenever you want. The main thing is to make sure you have some liquid assets before taking on more aggressive investments.

Currently, at least, the money market is not a bad place to have some money, because you can actually earn something. When you can earn 5 percent on your money that's liquid, you should definitely consider that option. Another option is co-investing with other limited partners in groups that aggregate storage units all over the country. You invest money up front, they use that money to buy independent storage units around the country until they get a certain critical mass, and then they sell them to the public. This way, investors can generate monthly income of 5–10 percent of their investment, and when they sell, they can double their original investment. The idea is to earn income while they're maturing, and when they're sold later, to enjoy capital gains. You can't go headlong into these kinds of investments because real estate has a downside, too. They are, however, decent options, and I know managers to whom I refer people if it's a good fit.

There are also independent wealth managers who can help people who want to keep a portion of their assets in the market, who have a sense of their commitment to keep their client safe, generate some income, but still have some significant growth opportunities. Insurance of different kinds is also a very important piece of the puzzle, including long-term care insurance and varieties of life insurance, which often make sense in combination with annuities.

My goal is not to put 100 percent of a client's money in annuities because that's not the right thing for everyone. I've dealt with some people who didn't have enough money saved and couldn't afford to take any risk. They had to maximize their future income using annuities and Social Security. For some clients, we suggest a reverse mortgage to provide an additional source of money, which can be a meaningful part of a retirement plan in the right circumstances.

There are all kinds of combinations and options that work for people in different positions with different sets of assets. If a person has $10 million and they lose a third of it, and they only need a couple hundred thousand dollars a year to live on, in combination with Social Security, they can take the risk. It would be prudent to allocate what they might have considered in bonds to fixed indexed annuities, but for someone like that, taking too much risk is less of a concern. My job is to help each individual or family make the best choices to right-size their risk and enjoy a meaningful retirement.

## Mr. Carlson's (Not-So) Risky Business

Mr. Carlson was a client of mine who was looking to fine-tune his risk a bit, and I was able to help him and his wife right-size their risk. A few years ago, Mr. Carlson sold his marketing company. He did well in that exit since it was a successful business, but he was going to continue working because his fellow leaders wanted him to stay and help run the company for as long as he wanted.

Mr. Carlson had a meaningful seven-figure portfolio from the sale of his business. He was continuing to make good money. He and his wife had no dependents. They were looking forward to traveling but were uncertain about exactly how long he was going to work, and that uncertainty was their main concern because they were in their sixties.

He had a professional managing his equity portfolio, but he wanted to have a certain amount of guaranteed income that they could rely on in addition to Social Security. This was their request; they wanted to right-size their risk. Because of all this, we arranged a laddering system for them.

How does laddering work? One major benefit of annuities is that each year you delay collecting your annuity payments, the amount of guaranteed lifetime income you receive from the annuity goes up. This is important to understand. Different plans are structured differently, but every year you defer collection of your income, it rises higher and higher. That meant the Carlsons could buy five different annuities with different dates to start collecting their income. When the first date arrived, they could collect from one annuity, then after a couple of years, they could start collecting it from another one. A couple more years later, they could start collecting from the third one, and so on. Over time, their yearly income from annuities increased.

We used about $500,000 to buy five annuities and create this income. As their needs increased over time (likely because Mr. Carlson would be working less and less as the years passed), they could gradually start bringing in more annuity income and let the remaining annuities continue to grow. They didn't know what the future would hold health-wise, or really in any other way, so they didn't know whether they would need the income all at once or in phases. In the end, it suited them very well to plan when to start collecting income from the next annuity and to raise their future income by waiting to collect on the others. They will be getting Social Security along the way and building their income by laddering.

This plan enabled them to grow a larger income than they might have otherwise had. If they had just put all their money into one annuity and had to start collecting all the promised payments at one time, it wouldn't be as advantageous. But instead they could decide to build their income in stages over a period of years, which helps them fine-tune their income for their specific needs. They had the flexibility to elect to start the income on each policy whenever they chose, without having to decide at the time of purchase.

Once the system is turned on, they get a monthly direct deposit in their bank account and a monthly Social Security payment while they're traveling. They can pay their bills online and travel, enjoying their life and retirement. With the work that Mr. Carlson continued doing, he was able to delay turning that income on for several years. We turned it on at different points in time so it added to the base income from Social Security, which is a major consideration for many of my clients. The remaining annuities continued to grow, and he still had a substantially larger amount under the care of an investment manager. We put only a portion of his money into annuities, but it satisfied their needs to have that floor of income they could rely on, and we were able to almost exactly right-size their risk, given their unique circumstances.

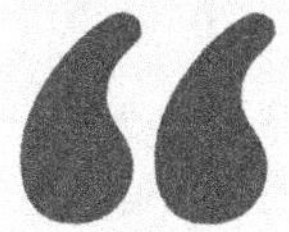

This approach ensures the amount of risk you're taking on matches your personality, circumstances, assets, and definition of a meaningful retirement.

The Carlsons didn't have to worry about the performance of the investment manager. They could always change managers if they wanted to, but they had plenty of cushion. They had enough money, but the laddering helped mitigate their reliance on the performance of that equity portfolio. Money managers can't give any guarantees or assurances that you won't lose principal along the way, so our approach worked out well.

This story shows how annuities have evolved over time and that there are some outstanding instruments to help people improve their lives, satisfaction, and peace of mind in retirement.

## Next Steps

If you want to manage your risk, "right-size" your risk, and calibrate your income and your exposure to the ups and downs of the market, then consider putting a portion of your principal into safe money annuities for income and for safer growth. This approach ensures the amount of risk you're taking on matches your personality, circumstances, assets, and definition of a meaningful retirement. This is what it looks like to clear the hurdle of risk, which is a major concern for many people nearing retirement. But others considering how to finish strong and live the best version of their retirement are most concerned with the hurdle of timing.

**CHAPTER 3**

# Clearing the Hurdle of Timing

The hurdle of timing is one of the trickiest barriers to a meaningful retirement. Just like in actual hurdles races, if you get your timing wrong, you can easily end up on your face in the dirt. The problem is that timing your retirement, your investments, and your income is challenging. That's why, rather than trying to perfectly time your date of retirement, the date you stop working, and a host of other important moments, it's better to give yourself some flexibility, some kind of margin, so that you don't have to time everything about your life and retirement exactly right.

After all, in the end, we're not in control of many things, including the markets and our own ultimate timeline, and we would need to control these things to get the timing exactly right. So, how do we win ourselves some flexibility,

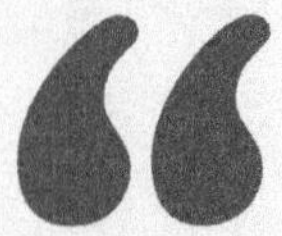

The problem is that timing your retirement, your investments, and your income is challenging.

a kind of timing buffer, so that we can clear the hurdle of timing and enjoy a meaningful retirement?

## Launching a Company at the Perfect Time

The feeling of launching a company at the perfect time, at the ramp-up of a nascent industry, is unique. We felt like we were able to read the timing almost by gut instinct. The excitement and exhilaration of that feeling carried us in the early days of seemingly never-ending work. What I was doing as a broker was placing companies into self-funded plans, and my business partner and I were having clients purchase catastrophic loss coverage, called "medical stop-loss," through the company he represented. When we got together, we felt like the only administrator in our area, because the only competition in town was another third-party administration (TPA) firm, and they weren't doing the job very well.

So we felt like we had a major advantage in a business that was just gaining traction in Houston at the time. Because of this timing, we felt highly optimistic that we'd make it work, and we hit the ground running. It was exhausting and stressful simply due to the intensity with which we were working. But because of the timing, there was never any actual fear of failure involved. We gained traction within a year. It wasn't too much of a struggle; the wind was behind us. We trusted our gut, worked hard, and followed our instincts.

The problem is not everything is timed so perfectly, and for many people, that's especially true of retirement. Not everyone can choose the perfect time to stop working, work less, retire, or start drawing on their savings or retirement assets. There are too many unknowns in business, in life, and in retirement, so we need margins. We need to give ourselves a buffer to clear the hurdle of timing.

## What Is the Hurdle of Timing?

The hurdle of timing involves unknown factors. When you stop working is important, and the market conditions in the first ten years of drawing on your assets are crucial. This leads to an important topic for people approaching retirement or starting to access their principal: sequence of returns.

Sequence of returns risk is the possibility that you'll lose money in your investments if the market suffers a downturn at the start of your retirement, which could compromise your retirement income. For example, the actual results of the S&P 500 since 2000 show how things can go badly if your timing is unfortunate. Coming out of the dot-com era, there were several years when the market was up big, double digits every year. It just kept rising to the point that people thought that old phrase, "This time is different." They thought we now had enough levers, between Fed action, fiscal activity, and the economists' decisions, that we just weren't going to have recessions anymore.

There was the actual belief that, if you happened to retire in 2000 and had a pile of money to live on the rest of your life, you could rely on the market to produce the kind of results it had been up until that time. You could draw on your stock portfolio for income, and it would sustain withdrawals for an indefinite period, even if your retirement lasted thirty or forty years. There was a kind of euphoria, and people believed they could make it work.

Well, they were wrong. Capital markets dried up. Start-up companies couldn't raise money. People were drawing down their principal at the same time that their investments were losing. We now know it was foolish not to have a more realistic plan.

Source: MacroTrends Historical Data, November 12, 2024, https://www.macrotrends.net/

Even today, we're tempted to believe the same old story. We've had such a run since the Great Recession in

2008–2009. The market has just kept going up, with only two minor down years before 2020. People have gotten complacent again. Many investors have felt like the stock market would just keep rising. People have been expecting to earn 10–12 percent a year. Those aren't realistic long-term numbers, though, especially given the fact that over time, recessions occur on an average of every five or six years.

Most people can't choose exactly when they're going to retire, and there's no way to know the future of the market. These unknowns are part of the hurdle of timing.

## Why Is Timing a Hurdle?

Timing is a hurdle because no one knows the future for sure. We're not in control of the future. We need to face that reality to make the best possible decisions for retirement. Because of this, part of my job is trying to get people to realize that if they're approaching retirement now, what the market does in the next ten years is critical. I try to help people visualize what it may do. If it's as bad as what occurred from 2000 to 2010, and people are withdrawing money while they're fully invested in the market, they can deplete their account substantially. This is why we talk about protecting that money, or at least a significant portion of it, so that it will last. That way, they're not losing principal in the underlying account while they're withdrawing money. People can avoid that by having a base of guaranteed lifetime income to supplement Social Security.

A guaranteed income will take care of their basic needs while they're still assuming some risk in other areas of their portfolio, and it can sustain them for many years to come. But if people are risking the loss of 25–40 percent of their portfolio and withdrawing at a "safe" rate of 4 percent a year, they can deplete their account in a hurry. Take the example of the dot-com bubble. If your portfolio was fully invested in the S&P 500, you exactly tracked that index for three years, and you were pulling out 4 percent of your starting balance each year for income, your account balance would be down 50 percent in three years.

In the example that I show my clients, we call this assessment a "stress test," and it's based on actual market performance. We look at making withdrawals, starting in 2000, that result in their account balance dropping 70 percent just by taking out 4 percent of the original amount. This withdrawal becomes mathematically more than 10 percent of the account balance at that time. On the other hand, we compare it to the approach of protecting a portion of their money with an indexed annuity that doesn't lose principal. Even though it doesn't gain any earnings in the years when the market is down, not losing money from that underlying principal sustains it at a substantially higher rate over the long term.

If you lose 30 percent of your account, you have to earn, before withdrawals, 43 percent to break even again. If you're taking money out for income, it becomes that much harder to recover. So when you're drawing on a portfolio that consists of investment capital alone, and you're losing principal along the way, it's a double whammy. If those losses occur in the early years, and you're trying to work your way out while you're pulling money out because of the mathematical reality I just described, you have to earn a much higher return than the percentage of your loss just to get even again, and that's ignoring the money you're taking out for income. It's like trying to dig out of a hole while the dirt keeps falling back in. It can feel like trying to escape quicksand.

Now, if you retired in 2010 and had a portfolio that you felt was sufficient to satisfy your needs, for the first ten years, it grew and grew. If you were pulling out 4 percent of what you started with every year, your account balance would be growing substantially over that period. You would be in great shape. Remember, timing is everything. The question is this: What are the next ten years going to look like? We just don't know. What's the market going to do tomorrow? Next year? Over the next ten years? These are questions we can't ever really answer. How long are you going to live? We can't answer that crucial question either.

Because of these unknown realities, we have to take action to make sure your retirement income is sustainable and not subject it to drawdowns that would ultimately create a crisis of running out of money. The thing is, for many people, it's entirely preventable.

### *When Do I Start Preparing for Retirement?*

The time to start is early; not in your final years of full-time employment as retirement approaches, and certainly not during retirement, unless you have money you can afford to lose and still maintain your standard of living. Start early, then protect your winnings. If you have some left over to continue to invest, then that's great; keep working with that portion of your assets once you've ensured you'll have what you need to enjoy a meaningful retirement.

### *When Do I Stop Pursuing More?*

It's hard to know exactly when to stop investing for maximum growth potential and when to start shoring up your gains because timing is tricky. What you can do is make a plan, start reducing risk, and create a buffer of income, and therefore timing. Then you don't have to get the timing exactly right as you retire, stop working, and convert a preparation mentality into a retirement mentality. Give yourself flexibility and margin when it comes to those decisions.

### *When Do I Start Protecting What I Have?*

For most of us, especially if we're approaching retirement, the best time to prepare to clear the hurdle of timing is now, while we have the lead. We make the timing of retirement less tricky and give ourselves space to catch up when we start to protect some of our principal from loss and the unknown future movements of the market. It's also a good time to get a portion of your principal into safe money annuities while interest rates are high (relatively speaking), so that's something to consider.

The bottom line is that the wise move is to mitigate your exposure to the unknown future of the market. You can use annuities and these safe money concepts to protect what you have from loss by providing a floor of income, which is what an indexed annuity is designed to do. These two features can supplement an investment portfolio, substantially enhancing the sustainability of your retirement account.

As I mentioned above, the first few years of your retirement are very important when it comes to protecting your principal. Sequence of returns risk could mean you suffer losses in the early part of the period when you're relying on your investments for income. Now, if you're not actively taking money out, the way the math works is interesting. The sequence of returns has much less impact on an account from which you're not drawing income. In that case, the order of the returns doesn't matter. You can take losses in the first three years and gains in the next few years. In that case, you would have a whole different set of models of gains and losses, and you could end up in the same place at the end of a given term. But if you're taking money out, it creates a critical problem in terms of the order those losses come in. It becomes hugely problematic if you're taking money out and those losses occur in the early years because of the

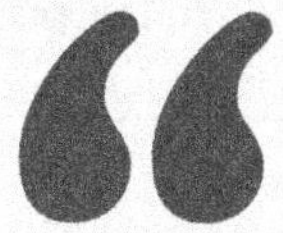

You can clear the hurdle of timing by building a buffer.

math we explored above. You're trying to dig out of a hole that's refilling faster than you can dig, so it's very difficult to climb out.

## How Do We Clear the Hurdle?

You can clear the hurdle of timing by building a buffer. Start to buffer your timing windows for your target date to stop working, retirement, shifting of your investments, and a whole host of other decisions by allocating a portion of principal to annuities that can protect your money and grow it at the same time. In this way, you give yourself a buffered *range* of retirement timings and options. Additionally, you can minimize taxes and maximize your income through strategic timing.

Remember our plan for the Carlsons: We laddered several hundred thousand dollars and planned to turn on their income from annuities at different times. However, we didn't know exactly when they would turn the income on because Mr. Carlson continued to work after selling his company. The laddering we set up gave him a great deal of flexibility in his timing. Tax mitigation also comes into play here because the laddering approach can be used to ensure you're not generating too much income at a given point in time, but you'll still have the ability to raise income to offset inflation. There's more than one benefit to using these kinds of tools.

Now, timing your income doesn't eliminate the huge unknown of how long you're going to live. We also don't know the future tax rates. So if we base a plan on our current tax rate, it may not work in the future. This is because, as many intelligent people believe, tax rates are likely to go up, if only because of government spending and the need to increase payroll taxes to cover impending Medicare and Social Security shortfalls. Additionally, the government keeps raising the maximum amount on which you pay tax. So taxes will probably continue to increase for a number of reasons.

There are several strategies to minimize taxes, involving tools like Roth IRAs (individual retirement accounts) and qualified charitable distributions, and timing matters for most of them, depending on your circumstances. Things can get complicated when you're timing Social Security withdrawals, putting money into pretax vs. posttax accounts, and dealing with changing tax rates. Then there's inflation and the details of how much and what kind of principal you're working with. But that's why having a plan that provides margin and flexibility matters, especially when it comes to timing. Ultimately, all of these things still depend on your individual circumstances; there's no one-size-fits-all approach. However, laddering income annuities provides layers of flexibility for even the most complex and changing circumstances. We ask each client how much they have and how much they need, because the retirement plans of two people with different amounts of principal and different income needs can't be structured exactly the same way.

## The Time of Your Life

When we talk about timing, we're not talking about funding annuities by "timing the market." Annuities are long-term instruments. Occasionally people feel like the market is too high and they don't want to put money in and have no interest next year because the market could crash, so they'd rather wait and see it fall, and they're trying to time moving their money into an annuity. It's easy to overthink the basic facts of the matter and end up on the wrong end of market timing.

I was using strategies one year expecting the market to fall, and then it went up for a couple of years although many analysts expected a downturn. This is why I encourage people not to overthink market timing. These are long-term strategies that win you the flexibility and margin to not have to worry about it; that's the point.

Mr. and Mrs. Robbins are around sixty years old. Mrs. Robbins is an accountant, and Mr. Robbins is a vice president at a medium-sized manufacturing company. They both have 401(k)s, and they're in good health, but they're not sure how many more years they want to work. They need flexibility.

The couple came to me so that we could put some of their money into annuities on a multi-contract basis. We put it into several different annuities that provide income and laddered them for timing and flexibility—creating a personal pension plan. The annuities were in the same denomination, but we issued several different contracts so they could turn on income at different times each year. The longer they wait to start collecting payments, the higher their income will be. This obviously helps them address the timing of when they'll retire and how much income they want to have when they do. We know today the exact amount of the payments they'll receive if they turn on retirement income three years from now. That number is contractually guaranteed today, and it's a handsome payout, way higher than a normal withdrawal rate. A key win here is that these plans pay a much higher amount than any safe withdrawal rate that would be sustainable in a portfolio. In some cases, it can be 7–10 percent per year or even more of their original principal as lifetime income, and there's no way they could get that kind of return by withdrawing from a 401(k) or IRA.

By laddering these plans, the Robbinses gain the flexibility they need and the comfort of knowing their future income based on what year they start the income stream. If they're in good health and they enjoy working longer, each year they delay turning that income on will raise the value of their personal pension plans. If one spouse wants to retire early and the other wants to keep working, they can do that and just turn on as much income as they need to supplement their working income. The Robbinses receive a lot of flexibility and comfort knowing all of this ahead of time. So from a timing standpoint, income annuities are game-changers, especially if we ladder them to allow people to build their income over time as they turn each one on separately.

On the front end of these plans, the sooner you set up an annuity, the better it is for you. This is because the deferrals are already known; you receive guaranteed credits on the growth amount that the insurance company uses to calculate the income. This means setting up the annuity sooner gives you greater flexibility in when you start collecting your payments. The Robbinses got the flexibility to decide that later. They don't have to decide the timing right now.

These are real people (even if we changed their names), and I can tell you they're thrilled to have the issue of timing put to bed. It's not something they have to worry about anymore because all of it is based on contractual guarantees. They know how much they're going to get, depending on what year they decide to do it, and they don't have to worry about losing the money at all.

This is especially true during periods when interest rates are up or even close to historic norms. A few years ago, we went through a period when the Fed had rates down under 1 percent. It was a struggle. The benefits that are now offered by insurance companies are substantially higher than they were five to seven years ago because of those extremely low interest rates.

Of course, in recent years, we've heard about the increase in rates, but they're closer to normal than they were several years ago because those were unrealistically low, pushed down by the Fed to help provide liquidity in the market. I don't see us going back to those days. So, moving forward, normalized rates should continue to offer opportunities for people in terms of their timing and funding these plans. Now, people like the Robbinses have a benefit of really attractive payout rates for income that they didn't have five to ten years ago when rates were extremely low, so their timing was very good in getting their plans funded.

Another thing to consider from the standpoint of timing is medical innovation. Part of the equation in these payout factors is life expectancy. If, lo and behold, a cure for cancer is discovered, or other things occur that would substantially increase life expectancy, that can affect the annuity plan. Every decade, life expectancies have gotten longer as medical technology improves and people become healthier. Ironically, that works against more substantial income payouts on annuities because life expectancies impact what actuaries are willing to pay out. Again, you want to buy yourself the flexibility and margin to free yourself from worry about these timing factors. That's what Mr. and Mrs. Robbins did, and now they've cleared the hurdle of timing on their way to a meaningful retirement.

## Next Steps

So, if you want to give yourself more margin for error in your timing, make retirement timing less tricky, and waste less time thinking about unknowns and future market conditions, then put a portion of your principal into annuities now as a buffer against the complexities and unknowns of

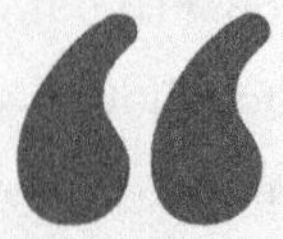

The sooner you clear the hurdle of timing, the more benefits you can experience when the time comes to enjoy your meaningful retirement.

the future. The sooner you clear the hurdle of timing, the more benefits you can experience when the time comes to enjoy your meaningful retirement. After all, timing is important, but a related question that many of us have as we near retirement is about the hurdle of exits.

CHAPTER 4

# Clearing the Hurdle of Exits

The hurdle of exits is not just about when to leave, but how. How do we move from one arena or era of life to the next in the best possible way? What are the conditions on the ground? What are the actual mechanics of moving on? The devil is in the details, and that's why it helps to have someone walk through your exit strategy with you—so that, as much as possible, you take your next step on your own terms.

## Knowing When to Leave

As I mentioned before, I was able to found, build, and sell multiple companies earlier in my career. The last company I sold was the largest exit, in terms of what we were paid, but we had a three-year earn-out. That meant we had to hit certain targets for three years after the deal, and we met those criteria. But by the time we did, I was bored to death with running the business, and there were some differences in perspective between the partners in terms of how to move forward, manage the business, and relate to each other as coworkers with new roles, now in the context of the much larger company that bought us.

In any case, I knew I didn't want to continue doing that job; it was clear that it was time for me to go. The money was good, and I could have made more if I had stayed on, but that wasn't the life I wanted. Sometimes there are non-monetary reasons to exit, and not every exit is that clear in terms of how and when to leave.

## What Is the Hurdle of Exits?

The hurdle of exits is the reality that we don't always get to choose how we leave something, whether it's a job, an investment, or another situation in life, and even if we do have the power to choose, it's not always clear how best to make our exit. Sometimes you get a pink slip. Sometimes you're forced into retirement. Sometimes your health fails and you can't work anymore. You don't have a choice. We would all like to be able to choose our own exits, but sometimes circumstances are imposed that aren't of our choosing. Sometimes you're given an opportunity you didn't see coming, or there's a change in your desires, goals, or vision. The need for flexibility to adjust to circumstances is something that people between the ages of fifty-five and sixty-five should be planning for.

For this reason, you may not want to have your money too much at risk during that critical period because you may have to start relying on it sooner than you expected. Frequently, when people are in their mid-to-late fifties or even early sixties, their kids are grown and moved out, they may or may not owe much on their house, and they're in a position to stash a lot more money than they were twenty years prior. They now have the ability to increase their rate of savings during that period, which can have a substantial impact on their retirement. Each year they delay retiring has a huge impact on the sustainability of their portfolio, but some people might not be able to make additional contributions to a retirement account. So if you're within ten years of when you want to retire, you should be planning actively for that exit because you don't know whether you'll be able to retire exactly when and how you think you will.

It's not always easy to exit, and that's true of many aspects of life. It does help to have a plan, though, and someone to help you put it together. You don't have to clear the hurdle of exits all by yourself.

## Why Are Exits a Hurdle?

At bottom, exits are a hurdle because it's hard to know when it's time to exit, no one knows the date of their final exit, and it's also hard to know the best way to exit.

How do you go about leaving the right way? How do you move from one way of doing things to the next? And when it comes to investment and retirement, how do you

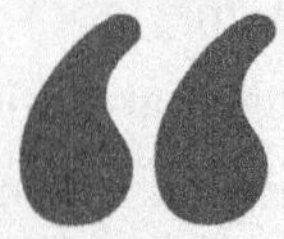

Positioning yourself, being honest in your preparation, and planning for multiple outcomes are all important to clearing the hurdle of exits.

know who to trust with your exit? Who do you go to for help? Who can help you plan for the next stage of life? For many people, it can be confusing, even overwhelming, to answer these questions on their own.

## How Do We Clear the Hurdle?

Positioning yourself, being honest in your preparation, and planning for multiple outcomes are all important to clearing the hurdle of exits. If you're expecting only the most optimal exit possible, you're leaving yourself open to being positioned badly when the exit does arrive.

An important factor here is the process of moving from one way of planning and preparing for retirement to the next, especially when it comes to investing for retirement. For instance, for many people it involves a 401(k) exit strategy, transferring some of your managed market investments into something a bit safer. Most 401(k) plans are invested in mutual funds, stock funds, and maybe even some bond funds. Substantial amounts are in target-date funds, which supposedly reallocate more to bonds than stocks over time. The statistics say, by the way, that indexed annuities are often superior to bonds in a portfolio, and once a person reaches fifty-nine and a half years old, they can roll their 401(k) money into an individual IRA and fund those partially with these annuities, whether they are annuities for income or annuities for growth.

Many people are limited to making allocations among the various funds that the 401(k) plan offers, but once you roll that over, you can better customize the allocation of those funds to suit your situation, whether that's dedicating a portion to provide guaranteed income later or focusing on growth and safety of the principal.

People who are still working can continue making contributions to the 401(k) plan and enjoy any match they may have from the employer on that money. They're not eliminated from being able to participate in the plan, and they can contribute as much as they want to, within legal limits regarding 401(k)s. For these people, it's a gradual exit that gives them the best of both worlds.

The process of liquidating some portion of a 401(k) and transferring it into an IRA is a careful one so that we don't create a taxable event in transferring retirement assets into annuities, if it's pretax money. If it's after-tax money, then they transfer that as well, but because they've already paid tax on it, they won't do so again. Having some portion of a 401(k) account in after-tax nondeductible contributions (not a Roth IRA) creates some reporting requirements that can be complex.

Ultimately, being prepared for the next step will help you clear the hurdle of exits more smoothly and with fewer bumps on the track, regardless of the details of your circumstance. If you know your options, seek the right guides, and maintain flexibility in your approach, you'll clear this hurdle to a meaningful retirement. Because of the flexibility they offer, annuities can help you exit well, whatever the means, methods, and timing might be. If you've been saving for retirement, particularly through a 401(k) program, then this exit will be a step into a safer place with more options to grow, preserve, liquidate, and diversify your assets and income.

## Flex It

Brad Noble is a manager in an energy company in Houston. When he was fifty-nine years old, he wanted to start moving some money out of his 401(k), years before retiring. He liked where he was, he liked the work he was doing, and he didn't necessarily want to leave anytime soon. He and his wife were about the same age, and they wanted to position themselves better for their future retirement. They approached me to help them allocate a portion of his 401(k) for future income through a rollover. His investment choices were limited in his 401(k) plan, and he wasn't comfortable with it.

He asked me point-blank, "Do I have to retire or quit work in order to move that money out?"

I was able to alleviate his concerns and reassure him that no, in fact, he could continue working there. In six months, he was going to be fifty-nine and a half, and we were able to lay the groundwork for making the transfers that would give him the flexibility he wanted.

The decision to move that money out was all about positioning him for that day in the future, that unknown day when he wants to retire. He was happy working for the time being, he simply wanted to change the way that money was

By positioning people with strategies that give them options, we help them escape plans that are so rigid, it's like having everything written in stone.

invested. So we put a portion of his principal into a couple of different types of products that accomplished multiple objectives. We also talked about when he would start drawing Social Security to optimize it. Now the Nobles have a plan with real flexibility, which was key for them, and they were very happy with that. The safety of their future income gives them peace of mind.

This peace of mind isn't necessarily only for retirement. You can have it even before retirement, knowing you've got things in order for when that day comes, as opposed to simply realizing one day, *My gosh, I'm going to be retired in six months!* It's a lot less stressful when you have a plan, and that's what we try to do for people: to make retirement less stressful and provide them with a degree of flexibility for that looming exit.

By positioning people with strategies that give them options, we help them escape plans that are so rigid, it's like having everything written in stone. There's also the matter of how much better the income can be if, like the Nobles, you start to move to safe money years before you retire.

Income annuities that place money on deposit today to guarantee what you'll receive several years out offer staggering returns in comparison to the portfolio growth that you would need to make a safe withdrawal rate from a 401(k). When we study comparisons of these income guarantees on a portion of a portfolio, the benefits are impressive.

When Mr. Noble gets ready to start his retirement income, if he were still planning on drawing down on his

401(k), he could take a safe withdrawal rate around 4 percent, and that would produce an income that would safely last him for his retirement, in all probability. But remember that 401(k)s are dealing in probabilities, which still leaves you open to bad outcomes. Annuity income, the kind that Mr. Noble has, on the other hand, is guaranteed.

However, even with aggressive appreciation on his 401(k), and taking only a 4 percent withdrawal, he would need something like a 25 percent compound rate for five years to build up enough wealth to bring in the amount of income that income annuities generate. That's not going to happen. In other words, it's much easier to provide future income through annuities than through a 401(k), especially if you allocate a portion of your principal to safe money in advance.

Remember that the years between when you place your principal in an income annuity and when you actually start using the income make a big difference; the more years you have left before you need the income, the higher the income will be. That's the advantage that the Nobles have. Again, they didn't allocate 100 percent of their retirement money to it, but for that portion, the guarantee is staggering. People are surprised at what they can get, especially with interest rates returning to normal, historical levels. Even if rates come down, they'll still be high enough to allow insurance companies to provide substantial guarantees of income into the future.

That 25 percent compound rate is a real example. The numbers aren't close. To be fair, it's not an apples-to-apples comparison because the 4 percent withdrawal would allow that person to preserve some principal in many cases, to provide a legacy benefit to whomever they choose. After about twenty years, the income annuity won't have any legacy benefit, but the income benefit is tremendous. The traditional route of building a lump sum of money and then making withdrawals on it can't compete with what people can get on a guaranteed basis in an income annuity. If that legacy benefit is something people still want, then they can preserve a portion of their principal, like the Nobles did, for that purpose. They now have the flexibility of income and legacy when it comes time to exit into the next stage of life. The path is now smoother for Mr. and Mrs. Noble, and the hurdle of exits isn't so intimidating after all.

## Next Steps

If you're planning your exit, consider putting a portion of your principal into annuities to gain flexibility and smooth the exit, ensuring a safer next phase as you step into a better future. With the hurdles of loss, risk, timing, and exits cleared, you can focus on the final challenge: the hurdle of retirement itself.

CHAPTER 5

# Clearing the Hurdle of Retirement

Wait—isn't retirement the finish line rather than just another hurdle? Yes, in a sense. Retirement can be the goal, but for many people it also feels like an obstacle to overcome, even if most of the overcoming has to happen in advance. Understanding what we mean by *retirement* is part of the challenge of retirement itself: thinking about what version or vision of retirement is for you and then planning for that vision. Clearing the hurdle of retirement is all about thinking through and planning for the next meaningful season of life so that you can enjoy it.

## Golfing, Hunting, Fishing . . . Is That All?

In my opinion, rocking chairs are not a healthy place to be in retirement. After a strong run of successes, I was able to retire early, but there was no rocking chair for me. I stayed busy, I had plenty of sources of meaning, and there was plenty to do even though I wasn't working full-time anymore. I had lots of time to play golf, hunt, fish, and do other things I enjoy doing. We still had family responsibilities, and I was still involved in some businesses, mainly through angel investing.

When my investments didn't turn out the way I had hoped, having retired at an early age, I needed to "unretire" to get back to where I wanted to be financially. I had to eat some crow and go back to full-time work. It was a challenge, not an instant recovery or immediate success; it was a growth process. Once I got some traction, though, work became meaningful, enjoyable, and productive. There were pieces of a "classic" retirement that I enjoyed, and there are aspects of working that are still very meaningful for me. These days, more and more people are looking to incorporate both of those things into their retirement. But not everyone has the same story.

## What Is the Hurdle of Retirement?

The hurdle of retirement is the search for meaning. For many, retirement is about slowing down and enjoying life more fully. For others, it's about focusing on a purpose that isn't necessarily connected to a job or career. This varies from person to person, which is part of what makes it a hurdle. For most people, a meaningful retirement is the result of thinking, planning, and focusing on the things that are most

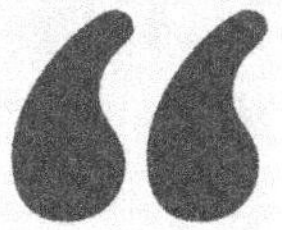

The hurdle of retirement is the search for meaning.

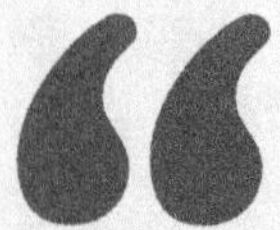

It's up to them to create that meaningful retirement, but I can help free them up to figure out what that looks like.

important in their life. However, the practical details of how to focus on those things can be complicated by worry, stress, fear, and financial reality, crowding out the pursuit of a meaningful retirement.

## Why Is Retirement a Hurdle?

For some people, retirement itself becomes a hurdle because of boredom; they just don't know what to do with themselves. People may wonder where their purpose is in retirement or struggle with a sense of meaninglessness, asking, "What now? What's the plan?" These are deep questions, and I'm not qualified to answer them for you. They take time and focus to answer. However, for many people, retirement is a hurdle because they can't even get to these questions, since they're constantly worried about a lack of income or they don't have the resources to live the life they've envisioned. Even people with substantial assets can get sucked into these worries.

Some people hate what they do for a living and can't wait to stop. They've got the day marked, they've got all these ideas about buying an RV and traveling. Others plan to keep working and never retire, and if they're physically able and their career allows them to do that, more power to them. So it varies with the individual. Are they ready? Are they anxious? They may be both of those things and everything in between. Many people find themselves somewhere in the middle. I tend to ask people who are excited to quit their job whether they think a rocking chair is a healthy place to be.

You can't play golf every day or travel 365 days a year, so it's important to know how you would like to spend your time.

## How Do We Clear the Hurdle?

Interjecting thought-provoking questions at least gives people the chance to think seriously about their plans. Some have better ideas and more plans thought out than others. People who have thought it through, whether they have a meticulous plan written down or just a general idea, will be a lot happier than those who focus only on not having to get up with the alarm clock and then ask themselves, "Well, what am I going to do today?" With no purpose, these people tend to sit around the house and waste away.

To be clear, I'm not a psychologist. I'm not a pastor. I don't have answers about the meaning of life for my clients. What I can do, though, is help take care of the financial part of their retirement, and to the extent that helps them sleep well at night and enjoy the time they have left, then I've contributed to their chances for a meaningful retirement. It's up to them to create that meaningful retirement, but I can help free them up to figure out what that looks like.

This is why I love what I do; it's meaningful for me. And that's the key: You can focus on the meaningful part of retirement when you aren't worried about income. Relationships, hobbies that build skills, personal growth, helping others, and meaningful work are all sources of fulfillment in retirement. Annuities can help clear the hurdles on your track to financial stability in retirement by protecting your principal and guaranteeing income.

There are a few other steps in financial preparation for retirement that have nothing to do with annuities but that I recommend my clients consider as part of their plan. Reverse mortgages and long-term care insurance are good tools. There are insurance tools to help you pay taxes on income from IRAs. These are just some of the tools available to people who want to focus on what really matters to them. That's my goal: to help free you up to clear the hurdle of retirement itself and finish strong.

## The Business of Retirement

Remember Mr. Carlson from chapter 2, who sold his business? He has done so well in his retirement. When he sold his company, we set up those laddered annuities. He's living according to his plan, and with the money he's getting from his annuities and from Social Security, he's able to make meaningful contributions to his church and other charities. The Carlsons are enjoying that part of the classic vision of retirement, but he also still uses his expertise in marketing to do a bit of work because it's meaningful for him and he's still very good at it. He has been living the balanced life: being able to travel, staying partially involved in the business, and generating some income without wearing himself out.

He can spend a small amount of time generating income, but he's got multiple other sources of retirement income to rely on. Aside from traveling, he and his wife are involved in social activities through their church and other groups, and they're some of the happiest people I know. They've really planned it well. He's even helped some other family members in their education and helped some people financially.

These stories are also important to me, because to see people positive and energized, enjoying a balanced and meaningful retirement, and know I was a small part of it means a lot to me. This work matters. I love putting the different pieces together and watching the plan work exactly the way we set it up. They cleared every hurdle. They're finishing strong. That's the reason I do what I do.

## Next Steps

If you want to focus on the meaningful aspects of your retirement, sleep well at night, stop worrying about money, and focus on the things that matter to you because you know you have a plan in place, consider investing a portion of your principal in annuities and take the next step toward finishing strong.

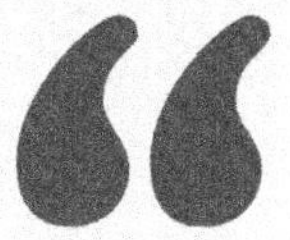

Even if we can't get rid of all the obstacles in life, when it comes to retirement, I believe we can clear some of them.

CONCLUSION

# The Finish Line

Life is full of hurdles: loss, risk, and questions of timing, exits, and meaning. No one can fully eliminate them, and I don't pretend to have all the answers to life's big questions. Many of us need a little help to clear these hurdles. A little advice, or even a sounding board, can go a long way. Even if we can't get rid of all the obstacles in life, when it comes to retirement, I believe we can clear some of them. With a solid plan and the right tools, you can take the next step toward a meaningful retirement.

You can eliminate many of the barriers to your meaningful retirement through strategic planning, and annuities can be a part of that plan

- to protect against loss.
- to manage risk.
- to make timing less tricky.
- to guide your exits.
- to help you focus on what gives your life meaning.

With a plan for financial stability, you can finish strong and win the race. Whether you're hoping to protect a portion of your principal, guard against market volatility and losses, right-size your risk, diversify your portfolio, grow your nest egg responsibly while eliminating downside, guarantee future income, design a personal pension plan, or give yourself a time and money buffer, safe money annuities can help you get where you want to go.

So if you want to clear the hurdles to a meaningful retirement, finish strong, win your race, and gain peace of mind and some guaranteed income, annuities might be just what you need, and I can help you take your next step. Don't hesitate to reach out today.

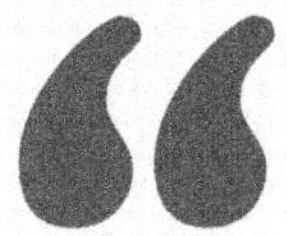

With a plan for financial stability, you can finish strong and win the race.

**FREQUENTLY ASKED QUESTIONS**

# About Annuities

*What about posttax money? Is that taxed when I move it into an annuity?*

If you've already paid taxes on money you put into an annuity, you don't pay tax on the earnings inside that annuity until you withdraw them. Therefore, there is a tax deferral for what we call "non-qualified" annuities, which are funded with after-tax dollars. You've already paid the tax on that money. Additionally, while the money is still in the annuity, you're not paying tax on it, unlike a CD, which requires you to pay tax on the interest you earn every year whether you ever move it out of the CD or not. This is a tax deferral benefit of posttax annuities.

### *Will I be double-taxed if I buy annuities?*

You're not going to pay double tax on your principal, but the government taxes the distributions of interest you earn on the after-tax money you put into the annuity. It's taxed on a last in, first out (LIFO) basis: The last money in is the first money out, and the last money in is interest.

The government considers the first money out and any gains of interest until you reach a point where you're distributing the original principal you placed in the fund. Once you're distributing the principal, you won't pay tax anymore since it's already been taxed.

If you've had the money in the account for a long time and it's grown substantially, any interest you've earned on it will be taxable. That interest is treated as ordinary income. But you don't pay tax on your principal again; you've already paid tax on it. So there is no double taxation.

### *Much of my retirement assets are in a pretax 401(k) and traditional IRA. How will my heirs be taxed on those funds when they receive them?*

Rules for inherited retirement funds can be complex. They depend heavily on who is receiving the accounts. A spouse can inherit the accounts and not have to pay tax immediately, but they will still be subject to required minimum distributions (RMDs) based on their age. Different rules apply to other beneficiaries.

For pretax retirement accounts, someone will be paying income taxes on the inherited funds. For large accounts that are expected to remain large throughout retirement, we sometimes use life insurance to provide tax–free income to beneficiaries to offset the potential of incurring huge income taxes. For married couples, life insurance policies that pay off after both spouses die can be a very economical way to provide cash to cover those large income taxes from pretax accounts. For example, annual premiums for those types of plans are frequently about 1 percent per year of the death benefit, payable to provide the tax-free income cash to pay the taxes.

*Are annuities safe?*

Annuities are generally safe, especially fixed, indexed, and immediate annuities. They are backed by the insurance company's financial strength. Also, most states provide protection to policy owners of annuities if an insurance company fails. The protection is provided by state guaranty associations that make policy owners whole up to certain limits, typically $250,000 per unique policy owner. A married couple can protect up to $750,000 by structuring ownership in three contracts—one in each spouse's name individually and another owned jointly—thereby creating three unique owners.

*What are annuity fees?*

Common fees include surrender charges, market value adjustments, administrative fees, and fees for optional riders. Variable annuities also have investment management fees. Many fixed and fixed indexed annuities charge no recurring annual fees at all. However, they typically include potential surrender charges and market value adjustment charges for total surrenders during an initial contractual period, commonly five to ten years. Most of those plans allow penalty-free withdrawals during those stated early years, commonly 10 percent per year. Surrender charges contractually decline each year during the surrender charge period and are eliminated when that initial period expires.

*Can I withdraw money from an annuity?*

Most annuities provide for a penalty-free withdrawal during a stated period, which is commonly five to ten years. These withdrawals are commonly 10 percent per year. Policies with income riders do not impose withdrawal penalties on the income when income distributions start.

*What happens to my annuity if I die?*

It depends on the type and terms of the annuity. The traditional immediate annuity usually has a minimum period during which income is guaranteed, even if the annuitant dies before the end of that term. Most other forms of annuities provide for the payment of a death benefit to named beneficiaries of the account value in the annuity at the time of death. However, most plans also provide for a surviving spouse to continue owning the annuity at the original owner's death and receiving all the benefits provided by the policy.

*How do I buy an annuity?*

You can purchase annuities from insurance companies through licensed agents, brokers, and financial advisors.

*What is a rider in an annuity?*

A rider is an extra feature, an enhancement that "rides" on the back of the basic contract for an additional cost. The most common choice is an income rider, which lets you ensure the payment of a lifetime income from the annuity. The income can be guaranteed and written in the policy, or it can be calculated at the time you choose to start drawing income based on the interest earned during the deferral or income payout period.

# About the Author

Tim Davis is the founder of Davis Capital Corp. As a Certified Financial Fiduciary®, Tim explains how retirees and near-retirees can protect their retirement money from market losses while growing those funds when the market rises. In addition to becoming a Retirement Income Certified Professional (RICP®), Tim has earned the Chartered Life Underwriter (CLU®) and Certified Employee Benefit Specialist (CEBS) designations.

Tim has decades of experience working with clients to establish plans for annuities, individual life and disability insurance, long-term care, and retirement plans, as well as large self-funded medical, dental, and disability plans.

Tim is motivated to ensure his clients have peace of mind that their retirement funds are safe and that they will enjoy a steady income for the rest of their lives. His primary focus is to help clients with retirement planning and funding to provide retirement income and principal growth with protection from the risk of market losses. Tim specializes in providing his clients with meaningful growth through indexed annuities while also protecting principal and income security.

Prior to the creation of Davis Capital Corp., Tim founded several other financial firms, including a thriving life insurance practice, a third-party claims administration firm (the largest in Houston before it was acquired by the Hospital Corporation of America), and an insurance brokerage firm. He also partnered in the purchase of a large Texas dental HMO that was later sold to Protective Life Insurance Company. Tim's extensive insurance background and history as a successful entrepreneur uniquely qualifies him to strategically design and place insurance plans for a broad spectrum of needs.

For the last thirty-plus years, Tim has resided on the banks of Buffalo Bayou in Katy, Texas, with his wife Vivian. Together, they have six wonderful daughters, great sons-in-law, and fifteen grandchildren. When he is not helping clients achieve their retirement goals, Tim enjoys spending as much time as possible with his family, along with hunting, fishing, and playing golf. He is also a big fan of college sports.

Made in the USA
Coppell, TX
19 January 2026